Contents

4   Anyone can make Fun Faces

6   Things to do with Fun Faces

8   Standing Fun Faces

9   Hanging Fun Faces

10   Reflecting Fun Faces

11   Fun Faces with earrings

12   Winker Fun Faces

13   Swallower Fun Faces

14   Finger friend Fun Faces

15   Hand mate Fun Faces

16   Fun Faces from envelopes

17   Modelling Fun Faces

18   Talker Fun Faces

20   Fun Faces for parties

22   Animal mask Fun Faces

24   Bird mask Fun Faces

26   Robot Fun Faces

27   Carnival head Fun Faces

28   Printer Fun Faces

30   Going on with Fun Faces

FUN FACES

Written, designed and illustrated by
Michael Grater

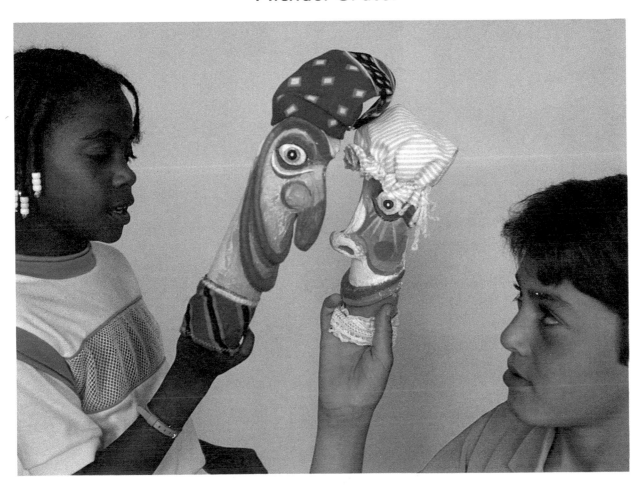

Macdonald

Anyone can make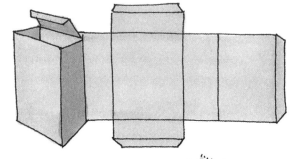

You only need a shape to start a fun face. Find an empty box or carton and open it out flat so that you have some good card to work on. When you have a shape you can add . . .

eyes . . .   a nose . . .   a happy mouth . . .   anything you like!

You can make fun faces in any shape you like.

How can you turn your shape into a face? You can decorate it with felt-tips . . .

or you can stick on bits of material. Start collecting papers, cloth, straws, foil, buttons, stamps, string, wool, sequins, and any other things which are thrown away that you could use to decorate your fun faces.

Try sticking on cut-out features instead of drawing or painting them.

You can cut into the edge of a shape.

You'll need a few simple tools to make fun faces – a ruler, scissors, white PVA glue, sticky tape, and a needle and thread. You should also collect lots of boxes and containers that are usually thrown away.

Things to do with FUN FACES

When you have made some fun faces from shapes you can . . .

put them on the wall . . .

fold them down the middle to make them stand up . . .

or you can hang them up by a thread.

You can wear fun faces as masks.

You can make fun faces into smilers, sculptures or ornaments by slotting them into boxes or cartons from your collection.

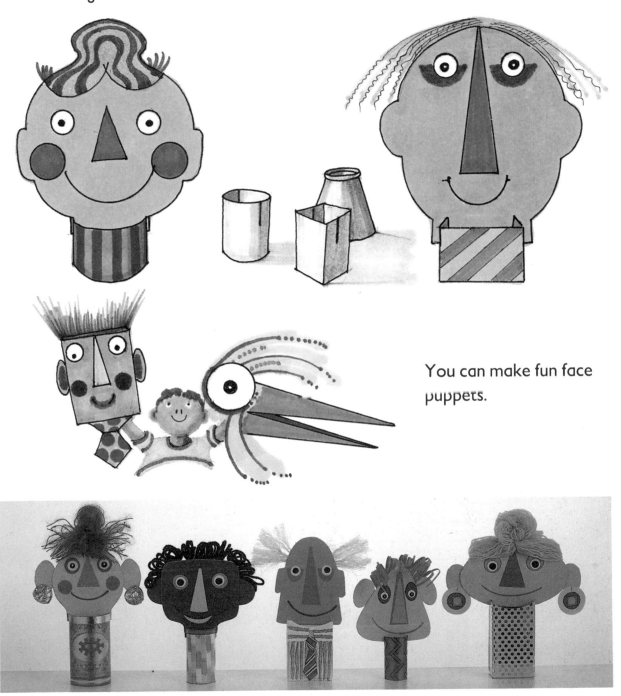

You can make fun face puppets.

Why not make some smilers to cheer someone up? Make one for a friend in hospital or some for your parents to take to work.

Standing  FUN FACES

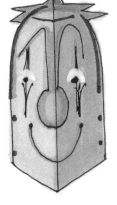 

Fun faces folded down the middle can be sent as cards to friends.

Score your card for folding by gently dragging the point of your scissors against a ruler held on the fold.

Can you make a tower of fun faces by slotting them together?

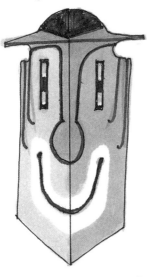

Cut some arches, a little larger than a ball, in some folded fun faces. Now you have some yawners you can use as skittles to bowl at. Each skittle has a different score, and you can work the number into the face on each skittle.

Hanging

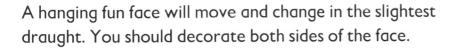

A hanging fun face will move and change in the slightest draught. You should decorate both sides of the face.

You can hang some fun faces together – as many as you have room for – to make a mobile, which is a sculpture that moves. You must start your mobile with the bottom shape and hang this on to the next shape up. Carry on like this until you have finished the mobile.

A fun face mobile can be arranged from lots of separate and different shapes.

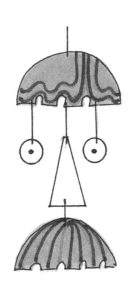

Remember to keep your mobiles simple. Wherever you hang them they will usually be seen from a distance.

Reflecting  FUN FACES

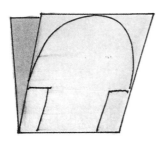

Why not make some reflecting fun faces or faces with hanging ear-rings?

How many ways could you reflect one face with another?

You can hang up reflectors or send them to your friends.

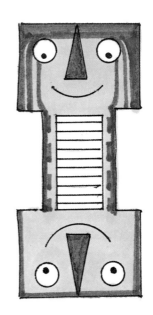

Perhaps you could write or draw something between the faces.

You could also make reflectors or ear-ringers that stand up by themselves. You could use cartons to make the happies and sads. Why are they called happies and sads?

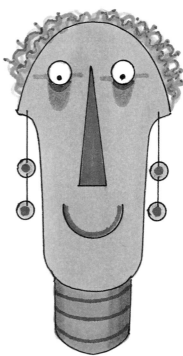

FUN FACES with earrings

To make ear-rings, cut some card shapes and glue them together. Spread glue all over the shapes and wrap them in foil, like chocolates. Smooth the foil over so that it sticks to the card. The foil shapes will reflect the light when they move.

Winker  FUN FACES

Cut out some card eye shapes and fix them loosely with metal paper fasteners to a fun face. When your fun face moves, the eyes will move with it and wink at you. You may need to reinforce the paper fasteners at the back with sticky tape. Better still, tape some transparent plastic lids to the face. A button or coin inside each lid makes a pupil.

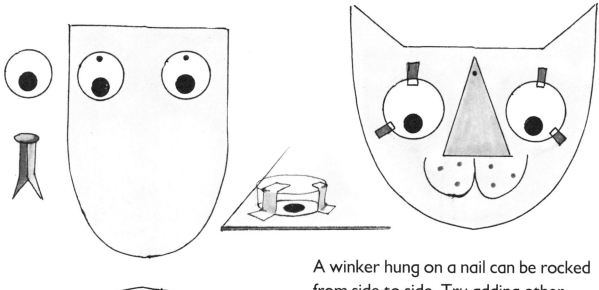

A winker hung on a nail can be rocked from side to side. Try adding other moving parts, such as ears or tails, on paper fasteners.

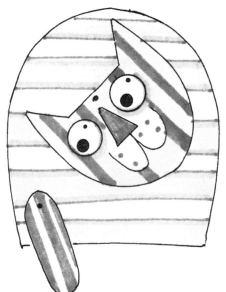

Swallower **FUN FACES**

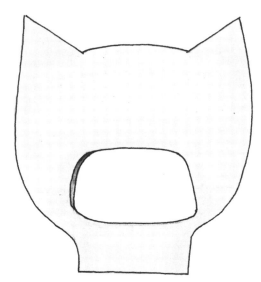

You can make a swallower by cutting a hole for a mouth in a fun face. You may need to ask an adult to help you cut the hole. Now cut another shape – an animal or a person – and hang it in the mouth.

You can make stand-up swallowers into animals or even monsters. Could you make a row of monster swallowers for your classroom? What could you add to your monsters to make them *really* frightening?

Finger friend FUN FACES

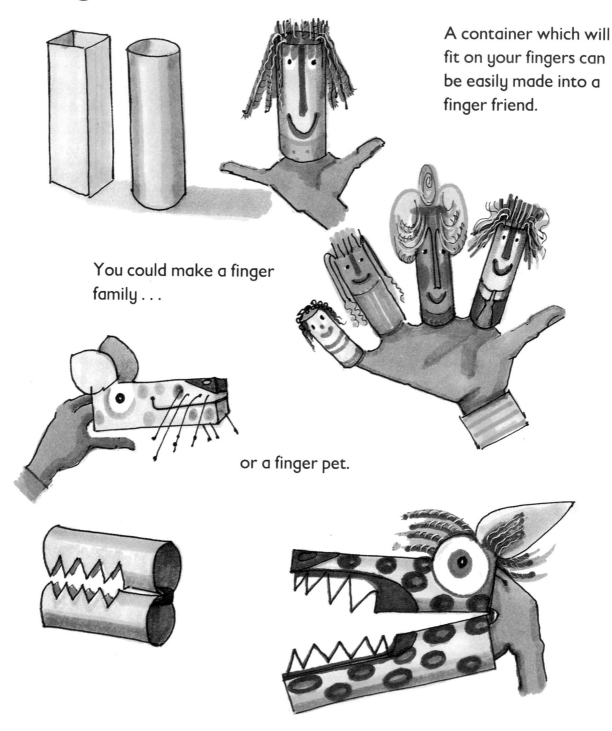

A container which will fit on your fingers can be easily made into a finger friend.

You could make a finger family . . .

or a finger pet.

If you tape two cylinders together at one end so that they open and close, you can make a snapper or even your own finger pet Jaws.

Hand mate FUN FACES

You will need a carton that you can hold easily or can wear on your hand to make a hand mate.

Draw on a fun face, perhaps add moving eyes and some hair, and you will have your own friendly puppet – a person, an animal or even a monster.

An old tie or some scraps of cloth will be enough to dress your hand mates. Try to find some string or wool for hair, especially string which you can fray at the ends to make it look more like real hair.

FUN FACES from envelopes

Every day millions of envelopes are cut open and thrown away. The strongest envelopes, especially the padded sort used to protect things sent through the post, can be made into all sorts of fun faces . . .

from fat and thin faces to friendly birds or animals.

You could illustrate your favourite stories or poems with envelope fun faces. Why not make some monsters and write some stories to go with them?

Perhaps you could make some envelope fun faces into pocket people that you can take with you if you go out.

Modelling FUN FACES

If you use a strong carton as a support you can model simple papier-mâché features on a fun face. Lay some newspaper on a table and mix some wallpaper paste.

Tear the newspaper into bits the size of your hand. Paste them well and squeeze them into a mixture you can model with. Fix the features on to the face with overlapping paper strips.

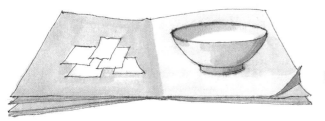

Don't make the modelled features too heavy. Make sure they are thoroughly dry before you paint or use the faces. Be sure to clear up when you've finished!

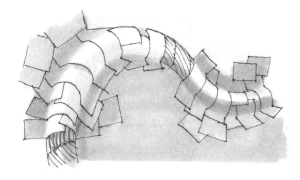

You can also add cord or thick string if you fix them with layers of tissue, pasted and overlapped.

Talker FUN FACES

You'll have hours of fun playing with these puppets!

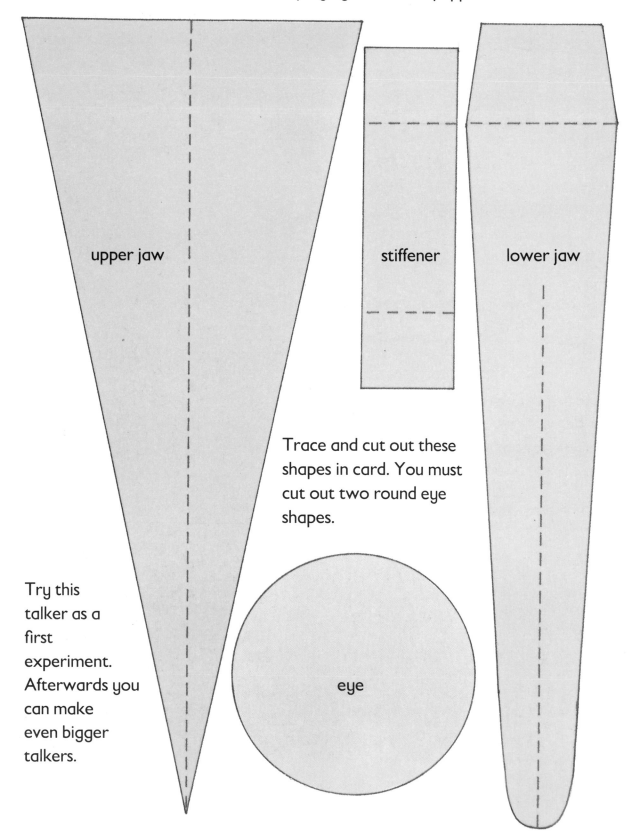

upper jaw

stiffener

lower jaw

Trace and cut out these shapes in card. You must cut out two round eye shapes.

eye

Try this talker as a first experiment. Afterwards you can make even bigger talkers.

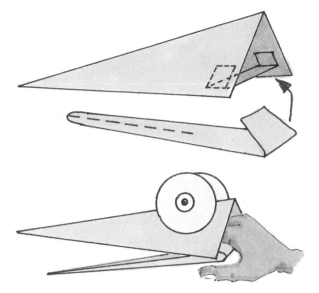

Fold the triangular shape and glue or staple it to the stiffener to make the upper jaw or beak. The lower jaw must be slightly folded along its length to strengthen it. Now hook it onto the stiffener and stick it in position. Glue or staple an eye on each side.

Use your thumb to work the jaw. When you've learned how to make your talker open and shut its mouth, you can use it as a puppet. Why not make some talker animals?

 **for parties**

Any material like card, corrugated paper, hessian or cloth can be used to make a party or carnival face. Mark out and cut holes for your nose and eyes.

 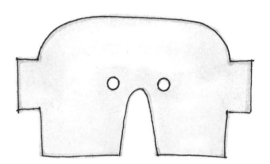

Think about your face's shape or how you could cut the edge.

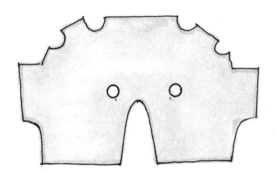 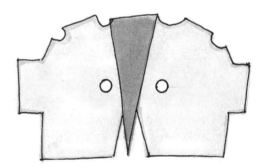

What sort of extra features could you add to your face?

Now find some ways to decorate your face, it's easy!

20

You can wear your faces by fixing strings or elastic to the flaps at the side.

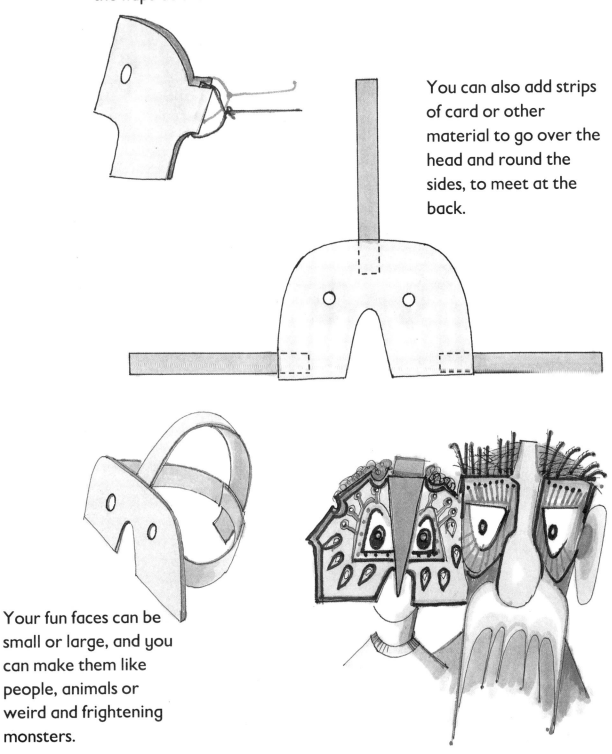

You can also add strips of card or other material to go over the head and round the sides, to meet at the back.

Your fun faces can be small or large, and you can make them like people, animals or weird and frightening monsters.

Animal mask FUN FACES

You can use the basic shape of a party mask to begin any animal mask. Add a few simple features like a nose, whiskers or stripes to turn it into an animal face.

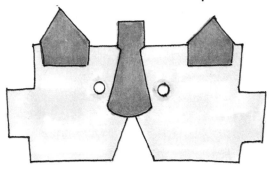 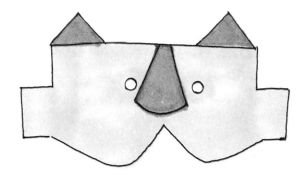

The cat family is particularly easy to model.

It will help if you start with a clear photograph of the animal you want to make a mask of.

For other animals you might need to extend the front of the mask so that it projects forward as a muzzle. You can use a basic shape like the one printed on these pages. Fold it through the middle to strengthen it and use the flaps to fix it to the main mask. The muzzle can be varied in shape to suit whatever head you want to make.

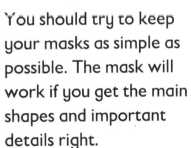

You should try to keep your masks as simple as possible. The mask will work if you get the main shapes and important details right.

Your mask will last longer if you cover the card shapes with hessian or cloth stuck down with white PVA glue.

Bird mask 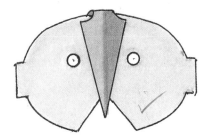 FUN FACES

As soon as you add a beak to a mask it begins to look like a bird.

 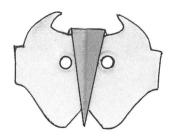

Library books will have lots of bird pictures, or why not visit a zoo to get ideas from real birds? Look at the shapes of the heads, eyes, and beaks. How is the bird decorated? Are the feathers smooth or textured? Try to get the same effect on your mask.

 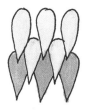

You can cut feather shapes from paper or cloth. Start at the bottom of the mask and layer the feathers on top of each other.

 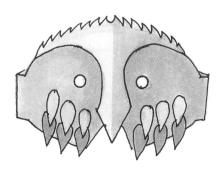

You can make a long beak for the toucan in the same way you made a muzzle for the animal mask. Glue or staple together the pointed end at the dotted lines.

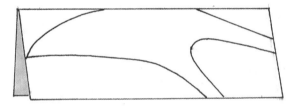

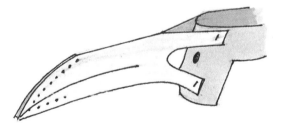

You could model this North American Indian mask in the same way. Can you find some books with pictures of different tribal masks?

Robot FUN FACES

You can always get good strong cartons from stores or supermarkets.

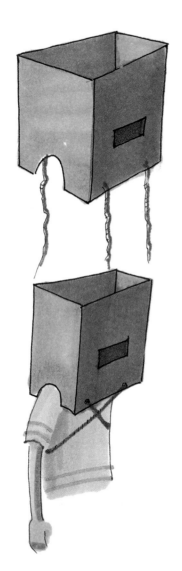

Cut off the top and bottom flaps of the carton and shape the sides to fit over your shoulders. Cut a hole to see through. Add strings or tapes so that you can tie the box mask on.

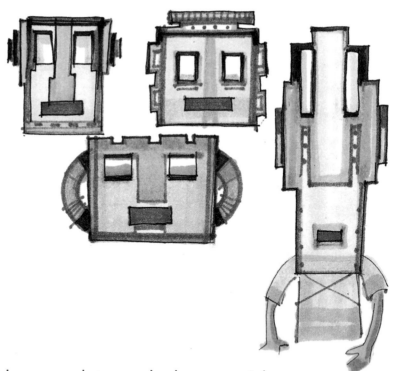

You can collect lids, paper plates, and other materials to add all sorts of knobs and devices to your robot masks. A tin of silver spray paint will give a metallic finish to the robot. Read the instructions on the can and be careful how you use it.

Carnival head FUN FACES

You can combine all the things you've learned making fun faces to make carnival heads. Make them on boxes, like the robots. Don't forget to add some moving eyes and reflective hangers. Add a little white PVA glue to your paint before you decorate your carnival heads.

Printer FUN FACES

You can use different shaped boxes, cartons, and lids you have collected to start a printing press. Lay a flat sponge or a pad of newspaper in a dish and thoroughly soak the pad with ink or paint. With this ink pad and the edges of some interesting shapes to press into it, you can print your own fun faces.

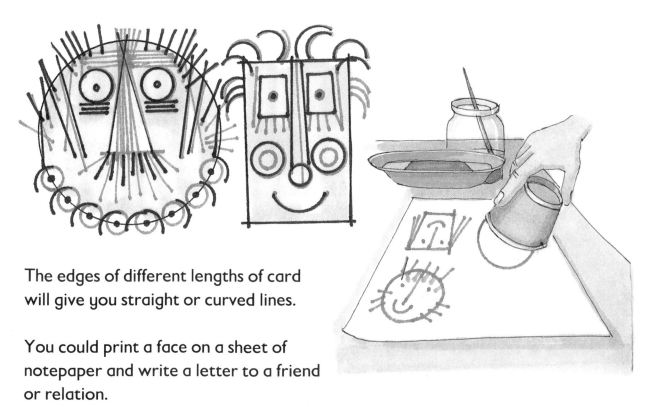

The edges of different lengths of card will give you straight or curved lines.

You could print a face on a sheet of notepaper and write a letter to a friend or relation.

Try printing your own gift paper on a sheet of plain wrapping paper. You could print the background for a poster to advertise a school club.

There are hundreds of things you could print –

a label for your own room door, greeting cards or even a sign for your classroom, with all the members of the class printing their faces on the sign.

Going on with FUN FACES

You can turn small boxes or containers into fun face tidies for pencils and felt-tips. Add some paper legs or tails.

A paper plate can be made into a calendar with bows that slide on pigtails to show the date.

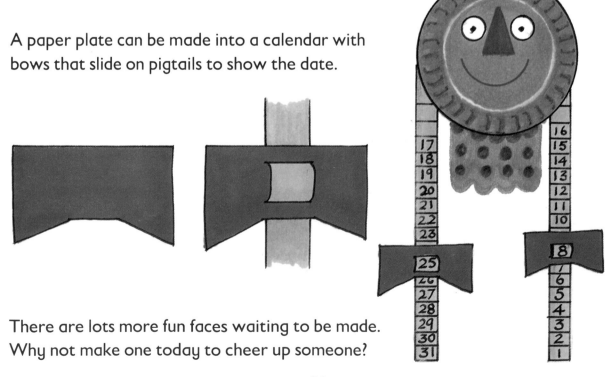

There are lots more fun faces waiting to be made. Why not make one today to cheer up someone?

Editor John Morton
Commissioned Photographs Corry Bevington/Photo Co-op
  Durrell Bishop
Picture Research Diana Morris
Production Ken Holt

Library Photographs
Barnaby's Picture Library: 24, 25b
ZEFA: 22

British Library Cataloguing in Publication Data
Grater, Michael
  Fun faces.—(Michael Grater's fun to
  make books; 1)
  1. Handicraft—Juvenile literature
  I. Title   II. Series
  745.5   TT160

  ISBN 0-356-11821-5
  ISBN 0-356-11815-0 Pbk

A MACDONALD BOOK

First published in Great Britain in 1987
by Macdonald & Co (Publishers) Ltd
London & Sydney

Printed in Great Britain by
Purnell Book Production Limited

Macdonald & Co (Publishers) Ltd
Greater London House, Hampstead Road,
London NW1 7QX

Members of the BPCC plc.